Happy Gloves

Charming Softy Friends Made from Colorful Gloves

Miyako Kanamori

HOME

I am a chipmunk who loves crafting.

Right now, I'm crazy about making stuffed

creations out of beautiful, colorful gloves.

I am first.

Chipmunk page 42

A girl wearing boots is second.

Girl page 44

Third comes a tiny frog who loves the rain.

Frog page 46

9

Brother and sister ducks are fourth.

Duck page 47

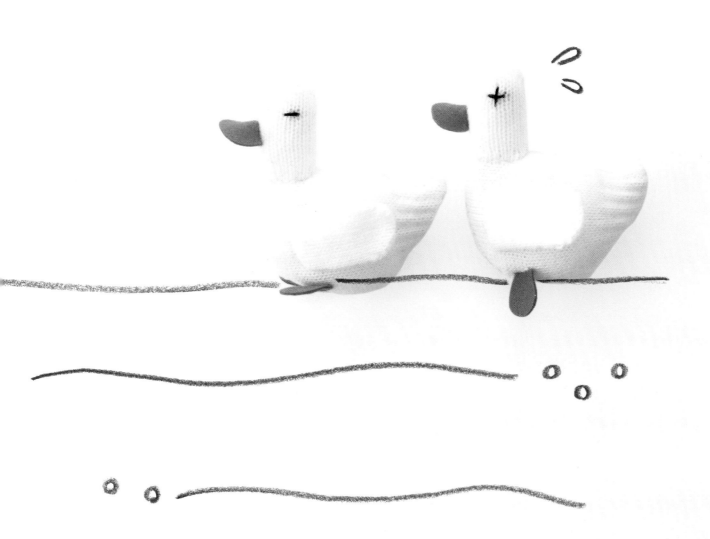

Number five is a sweet banana.

Banana _{page 48}

A large flower is sixth.

Flower _{page 48}

My friend the black cat is number seven.

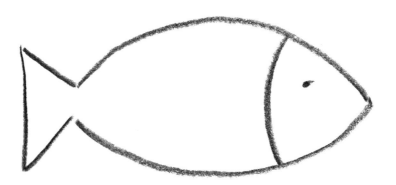

Cat page 49

A white-as-snow polar bear comes eighth.

Polar Bear page 50

Ninth is a bright red car.

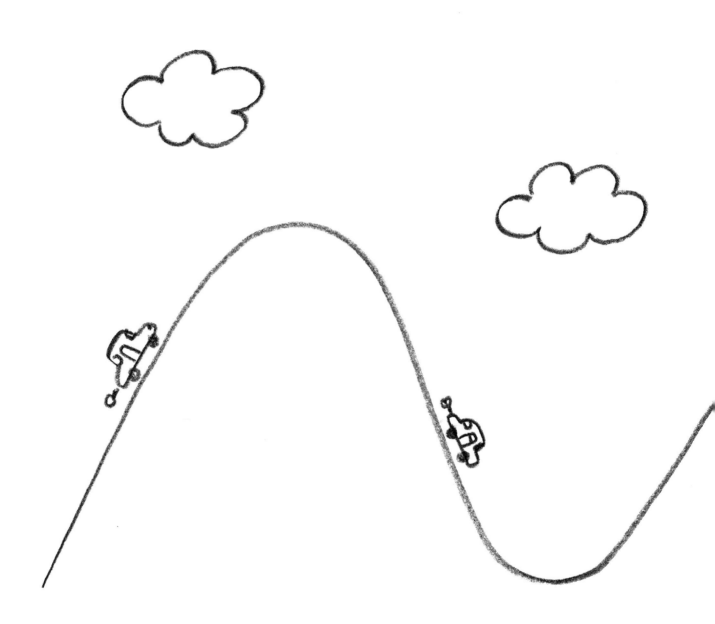

C a r page 51

Number ten is a sleepy-eyed donkey.

Donkey page 52

A strong, striped tiger is number eleven.

Tiger page 53

23

Twelfth is a penguin sitting on a block of ice.

Penguin page 54

An elephant with a long trunk is number thirteen.

Elephant page 55

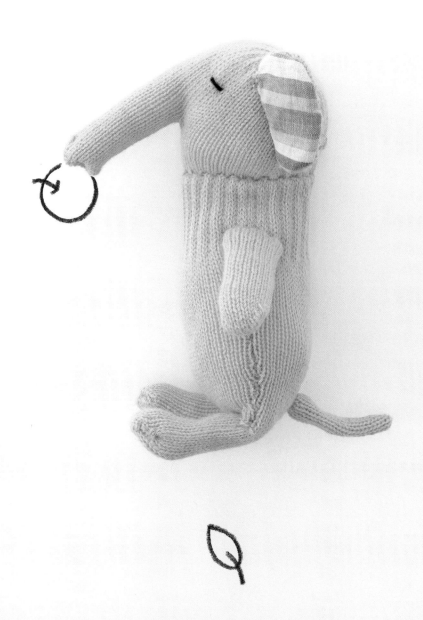

Fourteenth is a gentle lion.

Lion

Lion page 56

A mother rabbit and her finger-puppet babies are fifteenth.

Rabbit

page 58

A flower-trimmed teapot and teacup are sixteenth.

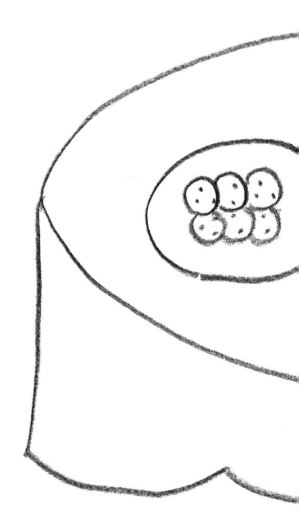

Teapot & Cup page 59

Doughnut   Muffin

Seventeenth is a doughnut, a muffin, and a slice of soft bread.

Bread page 60

Number eighteen is an overweight me.

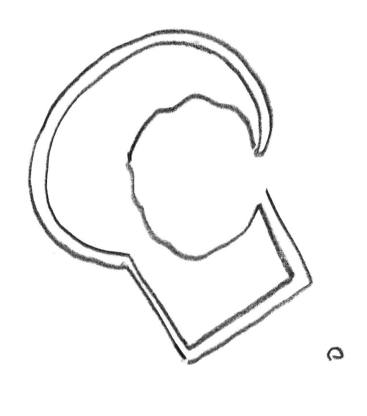

Fat Chipmunk pages 42, 43

Here are all of my softy friends on a mobile.

HELPFUL THINGS TO KNOW BEFORE STARTING

1 ABOUT THE GLOVE

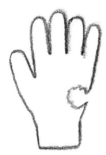

The gloves you use should be made of acrylic or another material that is elastic, because they will be easier to handle when creating these stuffed creations. Further, it is not necessary to purchase brand-new gloves; old gloves that you no longer wear are fine.

2 ABOUT THE THREAD

Yarn of middle thickness is easiest to work with for sewing together the stuffed creations and for stitching. A number 18 needle works best. If yarn is not available, embroidery thread or cotton thread is fine. Feel free to use whatever colors you like best.

3 ABOUT SEWING

Backstitching

When creating dotted lines, backstitching is the most secure, even when the area is filled with stuffing. Backstitching can also be used when creating a patterned stitch.

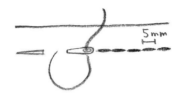

Vertical hem stitching

Vertical hem stitching is good when sewing the head, arms, and feet onto the body because the seams remain hidden. This stitch should also be used to sew the back of the head closed, to sew the felt portion on, and to sew shut the openings that were left open at the beginning of the project in order to flip the inside out.

Sew shut using a running stitch

When the openings of the arms, legs, and tails could easily be unraveled, use a thin running stitch ⅛ to 3/16 inch (3 to 5 mm) from the opening, then fold the edges inside, gather the thread, and sew the opening shut. This allows for a compact and clean finish.

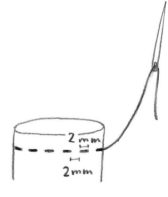

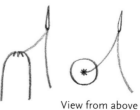

View from above

4 HOW TO FILL ME UP

Less (stuffing)　　　More (stuffing)

The stuffing you use for the projects can be found in local craft or fabric stores. Look for stuffing that's made from acrylic and has elasticity. When stuffing, tear a little bit at a time and stuff. When stuffing smaller parts like arms and legs, use the tip of a pencil to push the stuffing in. The amount that you use is up to you. Keep a close eye on the appearance while stuffing, as the amount of stuffing that you use can really transform the look of your creation. Less stuffing will make your creation more floppy, and more stuffing will give your creation straighter posture.

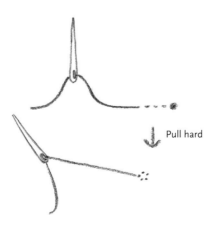

Pull hard

5 ABOUT BUTTONS AND STITCHING

Buttons are used for the animals' noses, but the size, color, and shapes of the buttons are completely up to you. The thread color used to stitch or sew the buttons on makes a big difference in the appearance of the final product, so have fun with it.

6 KNOTTING

The knot for the seams can be left on the outside because stitching and sewing on buttons takes place after stuffing. As an alternative, try the following: Insert the needle close to the starting area and bring it back out at the starting point. Pull hard so that the knot is pulled to the inside, but not back out. At the end of sewing, after knotting, push the needle back inside, and pull it out a little bit away from the end. Pull hard so that the knot is pulled back inside.

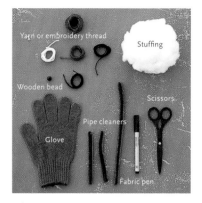

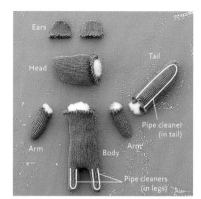

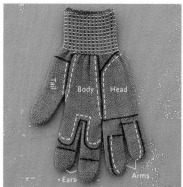

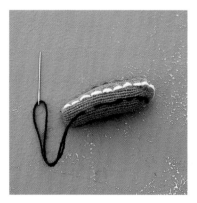

1

Materials and tools

1 brown glove, stuffing, 2 thick pipe cleaners (cut 1 in half), thin yarn or embroidery thread (brown, dark brown, white, orange, and black), 1 wooden bead, fabric pen, scissors, needle

2

Flip the glove inside out, draw lines with the fabric pen as directed in the diagram, and cut with scissors. After securing each part with a pin, sew along the dotted lines, approximately ⅛ inch (3 mm) from the seam with brown thread.

3

Flip each part right-side out. Bend all 3 pipe cleaner pieces into *U* shapes, and insert the 2 shorter pieces into the legs and the longer piece into the tail. Insert stuffing around the pipe cleaners in the legs and tail, as well as into the body, head, and arms. Do not stuff the ears.

4

Use a running stitch and sew the body, arms, and tail, leaving a ³⁄₁₆ inch (5 mm) border from the opening. Next, fold the opening inside, and sew the gathered area shut.

5

Fold the back of the head in the following order: left, right, bottom, then top (like a caramel-candy wrapper), and sew shut.

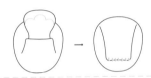

6

Gather the openings of the ears together, and insert them onto the back of the head. Sew together.

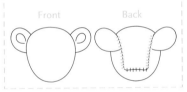

7

Use a backstitch to create stitching with white thread down the middle of the tail. Create the same backstitch in orange and dark brown ⁶⁄₁₆ inch (1 cm) on either side of the white stitching.

8

Sew the head, arms, and tail onto the body.

9

Use black thread for the eyes, and sew on the wooden bead for the nose. To complete, bend the legs to create feet and bend the tail.

The fat chipmunk on page 37 can be created by using extra stuffing in Step 3.

Girl page 7

1 Flip the gloves inside out, draw lines with a fabric pen as directed in the diagram, and cut along the lines. Sew as directed by the green dotted lines, leaving approximately a ³⁄₁₆ inch (5 mm) border from the seam.

2 Flip the body and arms right-side out. Cut a pipe cleaner in half and bend the pieces into U shapes, then insert them into the legs. Insert stuffing around the pipe cleaners, as well as into the body and arms. Fold the openings to the arms inside approximately ³⁄₁₆ inch (5 mm) and sew them onto the body.

3 Flip the head right-side out and fill with stuffing. Use a running stitch approximately ³⁄₁₆ inch (5 mm) from the opening, fold it inside, gather, and sew shut. Flip the ears right-side out, fold the openings inside approximately ³⁄₁₆ inch (5 mm), and sew to the head while gathering.

4 Sew the head onto the body.

5 For the hair, wrap a thick dark brown yarn around a piece of cardboard about 10 times, remove the cardboard, and tie the top part together loosely. Make 12 bunches.

6 Keep the bunches of hair in place with pins as shown in the diagram, and sew onto the head using embroidery thread. Do the same for the remaining bunches of hair.

7 Remove the loosely tied thread from each bunch and cut the loops of hair so that they hang straight.

8 Divide the hair into 2 bunches, each at the sides by the ears. Tie them together with yarn, braid, and tie the ends with more yarn.

9 Create eyes with black embroidery thread, a nose with beige thread, and a mouth with red thread.

10 Cut out 2 pieces of fabric for the dress according to the pattern shown in the diagram. Fold the curved neck and sleeves inside approximately ³⁄₁₆ inch (5 mm) and then sew. Place the 2 pieces together with what will be the outside facing inward. Leave a ³⁄₁₆ inch (5 mm) seam allowance and sew them together. Flip right-side out.

11 Flip a brown glove inside out and cut the index and ring finger portions as directed in the diagram. Use an overcast stitch approximately ³⁄₁₆ inch (5 mm) from the opening. Flip right-side out to complete the boots.

12 Place the dress and boots on the girl, and bend her feet out.

2
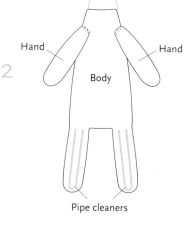

1
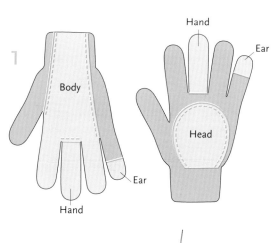

3
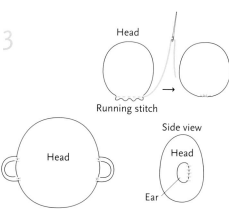

4
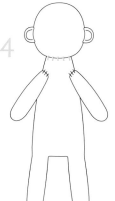

5
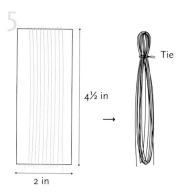

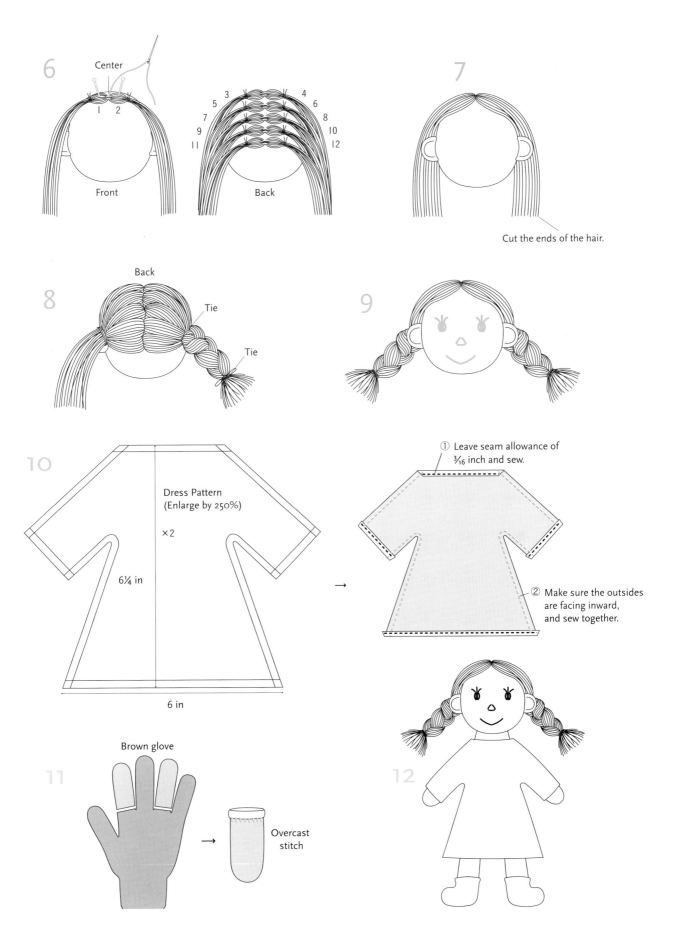

6

Center

Front

5 3
7
9
11

Back

4 6
8
10
12

7

Cut the ends of the hair.

8

Back

Tie

Tie

9

10

Dress Pattern
(Enlarge by 250%)

×2

6¼ in

6 in

① Leave seam allowance of
   ³⁄₁₆ inch and sew.

② Make sure the outsides
   are facing inward,
   and sew together.

11

Brown glove

→

Overcast
stitch

12

Frog page 9

1 Flip the glove inside out, draw lines with a fabric pen as directed in the diagram, and cut along the lines. Sew as directed by the green dotted lines, leaving approximately an ⅛ inch (3 mm) border from the seam.

2 Flip each glove piece right-side out. Cut a pipe cleaner in half and bend the pieces into *U* shapes, then insert them into the legs. Fill the body, the head, and the arms with stuffing. Do not stuff the legs.

3 For the body, head, and arms, use a running stitch approximately 3/16 inch (5 mm) from the openings, fold the openings inside, gather, and sew shut.

4 Sew the head and arms onto the body. Use black thread for the eyes, nose, and mouth, and bend the legs to create feet.

1

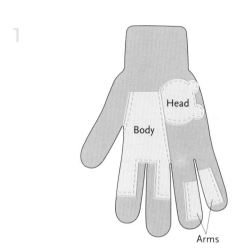

Head

Body

Arms

2

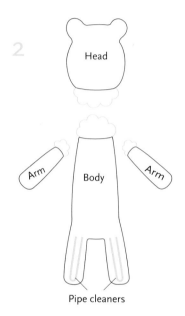

Head

Arm

Body

Arm

Pipe cleaners

3

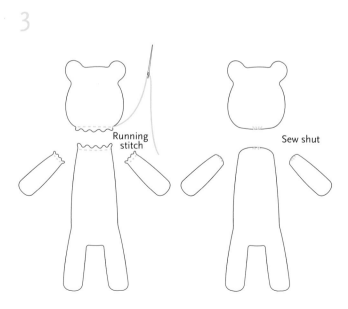

Running stitch

Sew shut

4

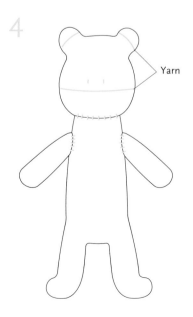

Yarn

Duck page 11

1 Flip the glove inside out, draw lines with a fabric pen as directed in the diagram, and cut along the lines. For the body, leave a ³⁄₃₂ inch (2 mm) opening, and sew as directed by the green dotted lines, leaving approximately a ³⁄₁₆ inch (5 mm) border from the seam.

2 Flip each piece right-side out, fill the head and body with stuffing, and sew the opening in the body closed.

3 For the body and the wings, fold the openings approximately ³⁄₁₆ inch (5 mm) inside and sew them onto the body.

4 For the beak and feet, cut yellow felt as directed in the diagram. Fold the beak border that attaches to the head approximately ³⁄₁₆ inch (5 mm) inside, and sew beak onto the head and feet onto the body.

5 Create eyes with black thread.

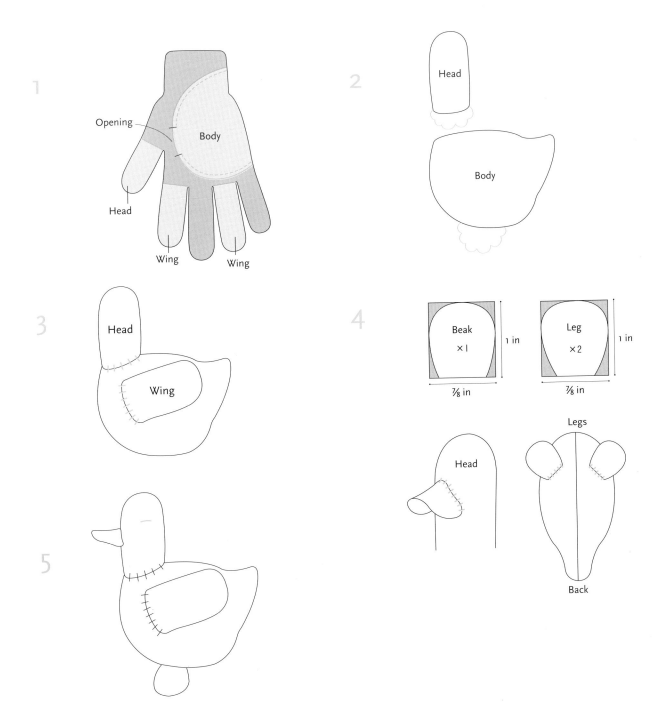

Banana and Flower <small>pages 12, 13</small>

1 Flip 1 yellow glove and both greenish-yellow gloves inside out. Keep the other yellow glove right-side out (the center of the finished flower will actually be inside out). Draw lines as directed by the diagram with a fabric pen and cut along the lines. Sew as directed by the green dotted lines, leaving approximately a ⅛ inch (3 mm) border from the seam.

2 Flip the banana and inside of the flower pieces right-side out, fill with stuffing, and sew the openings shut. Flip the remaining flower petals right-side out and fill them with stuffing. Flip the stems and the leaves right-side out, and fill the bottom of the stem with stuffing. Next, bend a pipe cleaner into a *U* shape and insert it into the stem, and insert stuffing around the pipe cleaner. Use a running stitch approximately 3⁄16 inch (5 mm) from the opening of the stem, and sew shut. Do not fill the leaves with stuffing.

3 Close the top of the banana using dark brown thread, creating a superimposed seam.

4 Place the flower petals around the middle of the flower, overlapping slightly. Secure the petals with pins and sew all around. Sew the stem in the center.

5 Fold the opening of the leaves inside approximately 3⁄16 inch (5 mm), fold in half, and sew onto the stem.

Banana

1

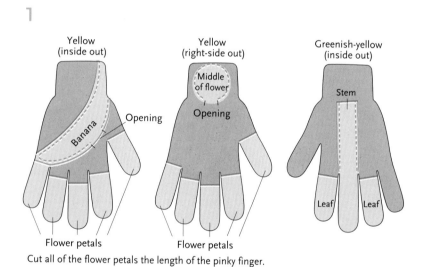

Yellow (inside out)

Yellow (right-side out)

Greenish-yellow (inside out)

Opening

Banana

Middle of flower

Opening

Stem

Leaf Leaf

Flower petals

Flower petals

Cut all of the flower petals the length of the pinky finger.

2

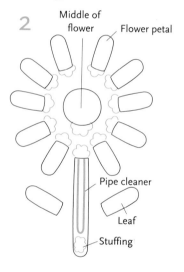

Middle of flower

Flower petal

Pipe cleaner

Leaf

Stuffing

3

4

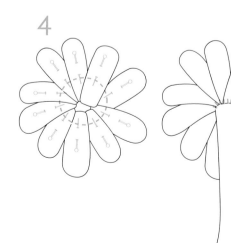

5

Cat page 15

1 Flip the glove inside out, draw lines with a fabric pen as directed in the diagram, and cut along the lines. Sew as directed by the green dotted lines, leaving approximately a 3/16 inch (5 mm) border from the seam.

2 Flip each area right-side out. Cut a pipe cleaner in half and bend the pieces into U shapes, then insert them into the legs. Insert stuffing around the pipe cleaners and into the body, head, arms, and tail. Do not fill the ears with stuffing.

3 Fold the back of the head in the following order: left, right, bottom, then top (like a caramel-candy wrapper), and sew shut. Fold the ears so that the peaks come to the middle, and sew onto the head.

4 Sew the head to the body, and sew the arms and the tail to the body, folding the openings inside approximately 3/16 inch (5 mm). Create eyes with white thread and whiskers with green thread. Use a wooden bead for the nose and bend the legs to create feet.

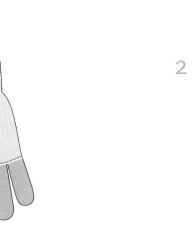

1

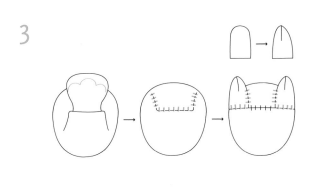

2

3

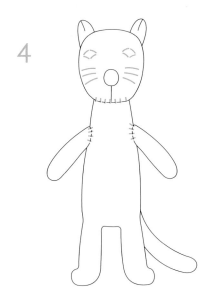

4

Polar Bear page 17

1 Flip the glove inside out, draw lines with a fabric pen as directed in the diagram, and cut along the lines. Sew as directed by the green dotted lines, leaving approximately a $\frac{3}{16}$ inch (5 mm) border from the seam.

2 Flip each area right-side out. Cut a pipe cleaner in half and bend the pieces into U shapes, then insert them into the legs. Insert stuffing around the pipe cleaners and into the body, head, arms, and tail. Do not fill the ears with stuffing. Use a running stitch approximately $\frac{3}{16}$ inch (5 mm) inside from the tail opening, fold the opening inside, gather, and sew shut.

3 Fold the back of the head in the following order: left, right, bottom, then top (like a caramel-candy wrapper), and sew shut. Fold the ears into the head, and sew together.

4 Sew the head and tail onto the body, and sew the arms to the body, folding the openings inside approximately $\frac{3}{16}$ inch (5 mm). Create eyes with black thread, use a wooden bead for the nose, and bend the legs to create feet.

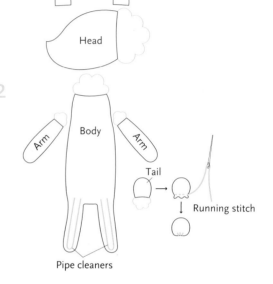

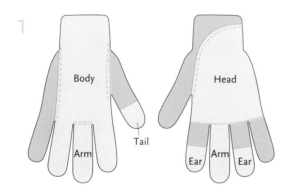

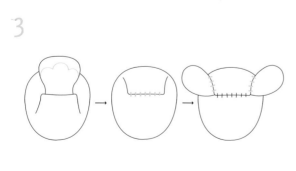

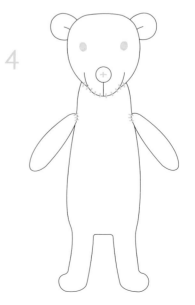

Car page 19

1 Flip the glove inside out, draw lines with a fabric pen as directed in the diagram, and cut along the lines. Sew as directed by the green dotted lines, leaving approximately a ³⁄₁₆ inch (5 mm) border from the seam.

2 Flip each area right-side out, fill with stuffing, and sew the car body shut. Use a running stitch approximately ³⁄₁₆ inch (5 mm) inside from the opening of the tire, fold the opening inside, gather, and sew shut.

3 In each of the areas where the tires were sewn shut, sew on a gray button.

4 Sew the tires onto each side of the car body, and create windows and doors by backstitching. Create lights using 2 yellow buttons.

1

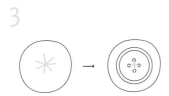

Car body

Tire

Tires

2

Car body

Tire

3

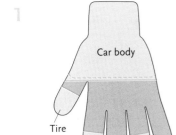

4

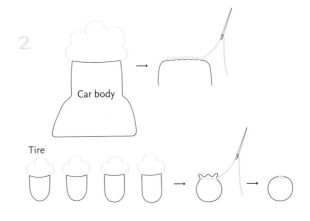

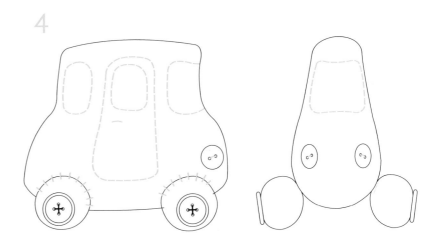

Donkey page 21

1 Flip the gloves inside out, draw lines with a fabric pen as directed in the diagram, and cut along the lines. Sew as directed by the green dotted lines, leaving approximately a 3⁄16 inch (5 mm) border from the seam.

2 Flip each area right-side out. Cut a pipe cleaner in half and bend the pieces into U shapes, then insert them into the legs. Insert stuffing around the pipe cleaners and into the body, head, arms, and tail. Do not fill the ears with stuffing.

3 Fold the back of the head in the following order: left, right, bottom, then top (like a caramel-candy wrapper), and sew shut.

4 Fold the ears in half, insert into the head, and sew together.

5 For the mane, wrap thick, black yarn around a piece of cardboard 15 times, remove the cardboard, and tie the bottom part together loosely. Make 8 such tassels.

6 Sew 7 of the tassels onto the top of the head, and place 1 on the end of the tail.

7 Sew the head onto the body, and sew the arms and the tail onto the body, folding the openings inside leaving approximately 3⁄16 inch (5 mm). Create eyes with black and white thread, create a nose with black thread, and bend the legs to create feet.

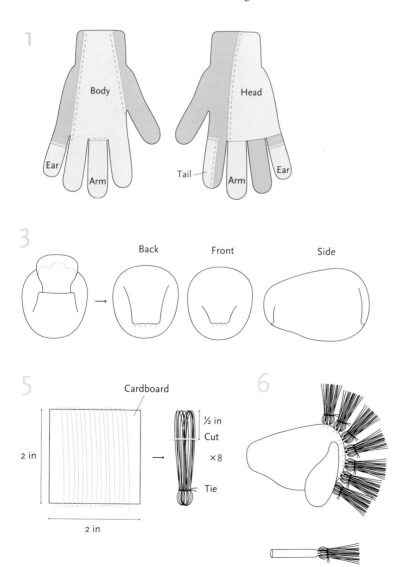

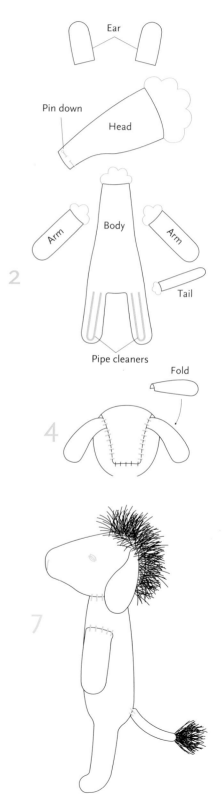

Tiger page 23

1 Flip the gloves inside out, draw lines with a fabric pen as directed in the diagram, and cut along the lines. Sew as directed by the green dotted lines, leaving approximately a ³⁄₁₆ inch (5 mm) border from the seam.

2 Flip each area right-side out. Cut a pipe cleaner in half and bend the pieces into *U* shapes, then insert them into the legs. Insert stuffing around the pipe cleaners and into the body, head, arms, and tail. Do not fill the ears with stuffing.

3 Fold the back of the head in the following order: left, right, bottom, then top (like a caramel-candy wrapper), and sew shut. Fold the ears so that the peaks come to the middle, and sew onto the head.

4 Sew the head onto the body, then sew the arms and tail onto the body, folding the openings inside leaving approximately ³⁄₁₆ inch (5 mm). Create eyes with black and white thread, and create a nose with a black button.

5 Create the horizontal stripes using thick, black, wavy yarn. Follow the numbered steps in Diagram 5 for guidance on creating stitches. Bend the legs to create feet.

Penguin   page 25

1 Flip the gloves inside out, draw lines with a fabric pen as directed in the diagram, and cut along the lines. Sew as directed by the green dotted lines, leaving approximately a ³⁄₁₆ inch (5 mm) border from the seam. Create the beak with yellow felt and the stomach with white felt.

2 Flip each area right-side out and fill the body and head with stuffing. For the head, use a running stitch approximately ³⁄₁₆ inch (5 mm) from the opening, fold the opening inside, gather, and sew shut.

3 Turn the penguin body upside down, so you are looking at the bottom seam (what will sit on a table). Fold the front point (the lower front part of the body) down and onto the bottom and sew. Folding the open part of the feet approximately ³⁄₁₆ inch (5 mm) inside, sew them to the lower part of the body.

4 Sew the white felt onto the body with white thread. For the wings, sew to the body after folding inside approximately ³⁄₁₆ inch (5 mm).

5 For the beak, put the 2 sides together and sew together with embroidery thread using a backstitch. Fill with stuffing and sew onto the face.

6 Sew the head onto the body, and use black and white thread to create the eyes.

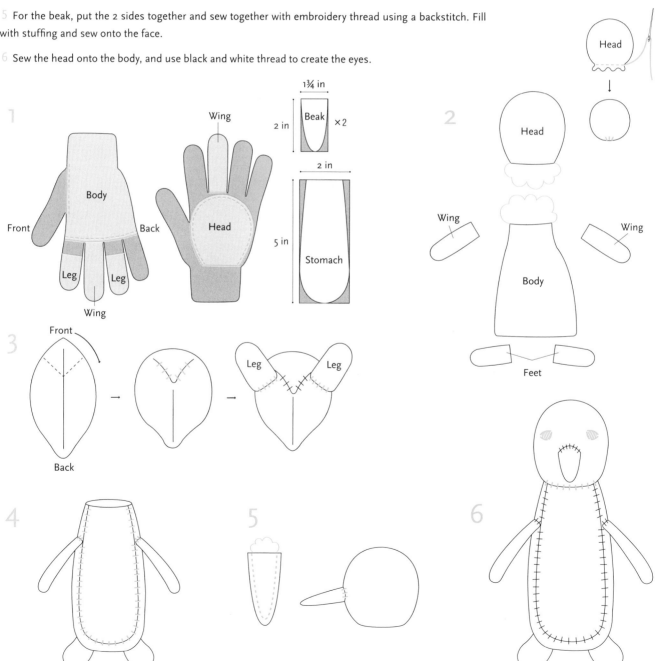

Elephant   page 27

1 Flip the gloves inside out, draw lines with a fabric pen as directed in the diagram, and cut along the lines. Sew as directed by the green dotted lines, leaving approximately a $3/16$ inch (5 mm) border from the seam.

2 Cut the ear parts open as directed in the diagram, draw a line with the fabric pen, and cut.

3 Place the ears from Step 2 on a piece of patterned fabric and cut it to the same size. Place 1 of each piece together, and sew together with embroidery thread using a backstitch.

4 Flip the pieces right-side out. Cut a pipe cleaner in half and bend the pieces into U shapes, then insert them into the legs. Insert stuffing around the pipe cleaners and into the body, head, and arms. Do not fill the tail with stuffing.

5 Fold the back of the head in the following order: left, right, bottom, then top (like a caramel-candy wrapper), and sew shut. Fold the ears into the head, and sew together.

6 Sew the head onto the body. Sew the arms and tail to the body after folding the openings inside approximately $3/16$ inch (5 mm). Create eyes using black thread and bend the legs to create feet.

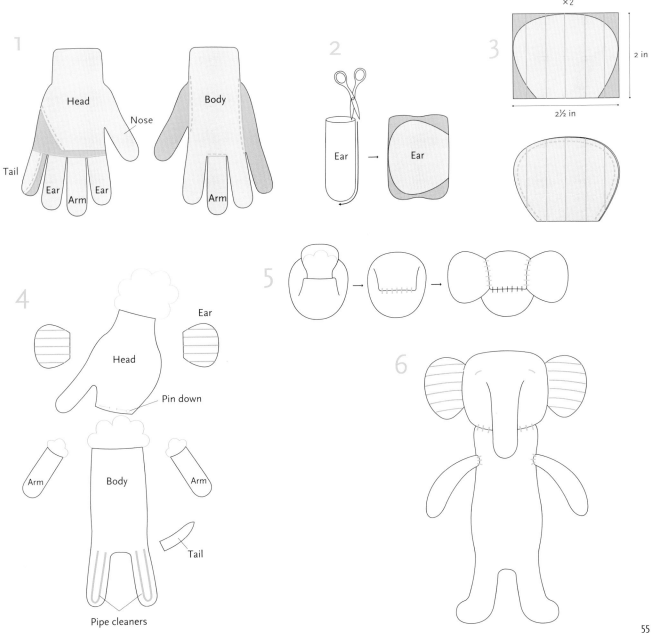

Lion page 29

1 Flip the gloves inside out, draw lines with a fabric pen as directed in the diagram, and cut along the lines. Sew as directed by the green dotted lines, leaving approximately a ³⁄₁₆ inch (5 mm) border from the seam.

2 Flip each area right-side out. Cut a pipe cleaner in half and bend the pieces into U shapes, then insert them into the legs. Insert stuffing around the pipe cleaners and into the body, head, and arms. Do not fill the tail or ears with stuffing.

3 Fold the back of the head in the following order: left, right, bottom, then top (like a caramel-candy wrapper), and sew shut. Fold the ears so that the peaks come to the middle, and sew onto the head.

4 For the mane, wrap thick, dark brown yarn around a piece of 2¾ x 2 inch (7 x 5 cm) cardboard 20 times, remove the cardboard, and tie the bottom part together to create tassels. Make 17 tassels. For the tail, wrap the yarn around a piece of 1¼ x 1¼ inch (3 x 3 cm) cardboard 10 times, and repeat the same process as the mane.

5 Sew the tassels to the head. For the tail, fold it inside of the opening and sew shut.

6 Sew the head and tail onto the body, then sew the arms onto the body, folding the openings inside approximately ³⁄₁₆ inch (5 mm). Create eyes with black thread and a nose with a button. Cut the mane to the desired length, cut the end of the tail, and bend the legs to create feet.

1

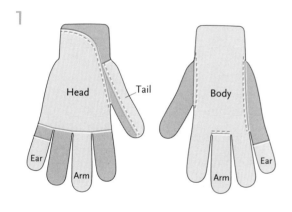

2

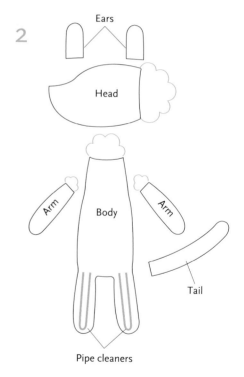

3

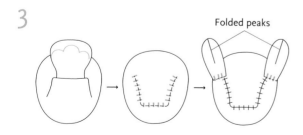

4

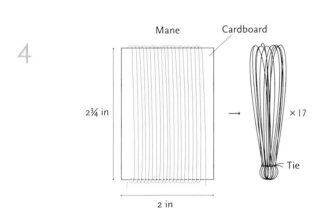

Mane — Cardboard

2¾ in

2 in

→ ×17

Tie

Tail — Cardboard

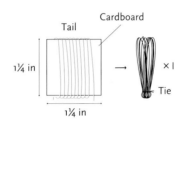

1¼ in

1¼ in

→ ×1

Tie

5

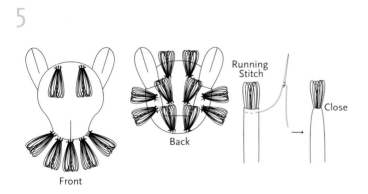

Front

Back

Running Stitch

Close

6

Cut the mane to the desired length

Mother and Baby Rabbits pages 30, 31

1 Flip 1 glove inside out, draw lines with a fabric pen as directed in the diagram, and cut along the lines. Sew as directed by the green dotted lines, leaving approximately a ³⁄₁₆ inch (5 mm) border from the seam.

2 Flip the head of the mother rabbit right-side out, and starting from the bottom, fold the bottom half inside.

3 Cover the opening of the body with the head and sew together. Create eyes with black and white thread, a mouth with red thread, and a nose with a button. Wrap a 12 inch (30 cm) long ribbon around the neck and tie.

4 Flip the head of the baby rabbit right-side out and fill with stuffing. Sew approximately ³⁄₁₆ inch (5 mm) from the opening, gather, and sew shut. Flip the body inside out, use an overcast stitch approximately ³⁄₁₆ inch (5 mm) from the opening. Flip right-side out. Sew the head and body together. Repeat for 2 more baby rabbits.

5 Create ears and arms using pink felt, and sew to the head and body using embroidery thread. Create eyes and a nose using black thread, and a mouth using red thread.

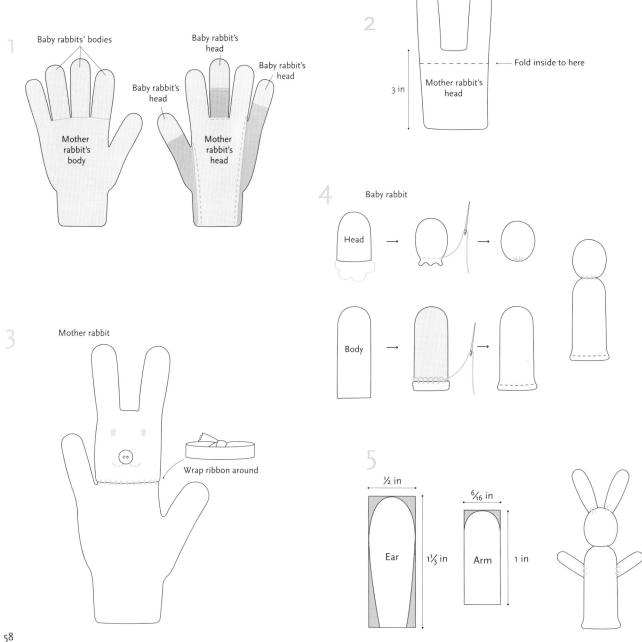

Teapot and Cup page 33

1 Cut the gloves as directed in the diagram.

2 Pin the openings of the teapot and cup, and fill the teapot, the handle, the lid, and the cup with stuffing.

3 Use a running stitch for the top and bottom of the teapot, gather, and sew shut. Sew the lid of the teapot, folding the opening inside approximately ³⁄₁₆ inch (5 mm). Sew the spout so that it faces up.

4 Sew together 2 teapot handles, fold the opening inside approximately ³⁄₁₆ inch (5 mm) and sew to the teapot.

5 Use a running stitch for the bottom of the cup, and sew shut. Fold the upper part inside so that it turns into the shape of a cup. Raise the handle and sew it to the top of the cup.

6 Sew a ribbon with embroidery thread to the teapot and cup (8 inches [20 cm] for the teapot and 9¾ inches [25 cm] for the cup).

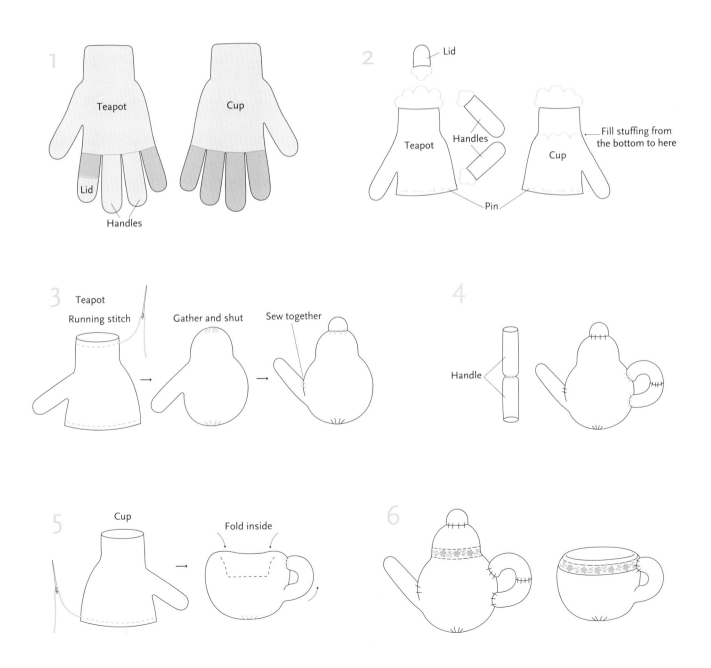

Doughnut, Muffin, and Bread pages 34, 35

1 Flip the gloves inside out, draw lines with a fabric pen as directed in the diagram, and cut along the lines. Sew as directed by the green dotted lines, leaving approximately a ³⁄₁₆ inch (5 mm) border from the seam.

2 Flip each area right-side out and fill with stuffing.

3 Sew shut the openings to the bread and muffin. Use a running stitch for each doughnut part, leaving approximately ³⁄₁₆ inch (5 mm) from the opening. Fold each opening inside, gather, and sew shut.

4 Cut a piece of white felt approximately ³⁄₁₆ inch (5 mm) smaller than the bread, and sew onto the bread.

5 Sew wooden beads onto the muffin.

6 Use an overcast stitch to connect the 5 doughnut pieces to make the whole doughnut.

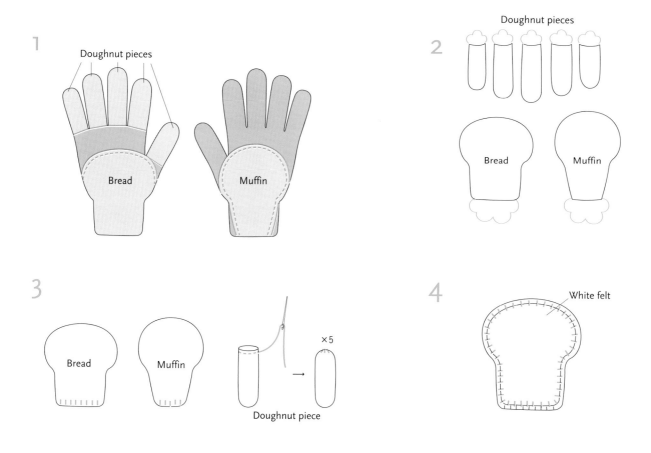

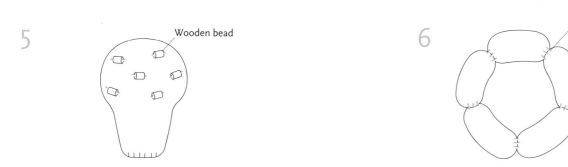

HOW TO STITCH THE FACE

Follow the numbered steps in the diagrams for guidance on creating the stitches.

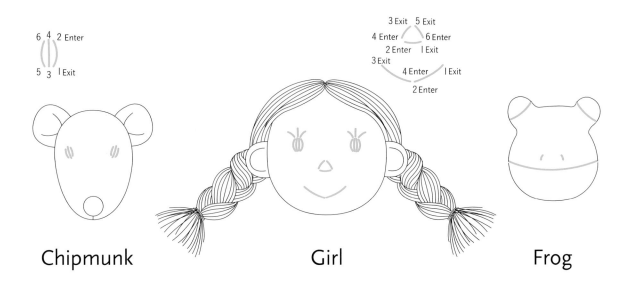

Chipmunk

Girl

Frog

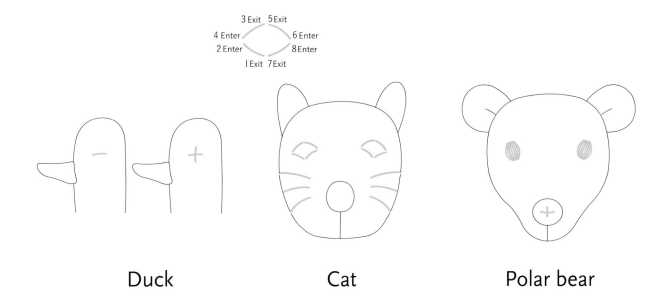

Duck

Cat

Polar bear

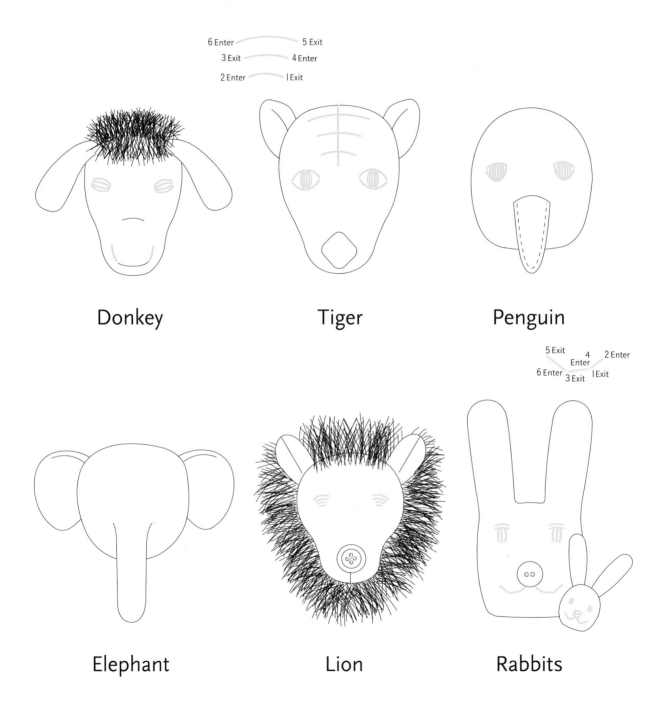

6 Enter   5 Exit
3 Exit   4 Enter
2 Enter   I Exit

Donkey   Tiger   Penguin

5 Exit   4   2 Enter
    Enter
6 Enter   3 Exit   I Exit

Elephant   Lion   Rabbits